CHANGE YOUR LIFE

LIVING THE WISDOM OF THE WORD

By

Blaise Tshibwabwa

© Copyright 2024 by Blaise Tshibwabwa – All rights reserved. It is not legal to reproduce, duplicate, or transmit any part of this document in either electronic means or printed format. Recording of this publications is strictly prohibited.

ISBN: 978-1-7779515-7-3

This book is dedicated to:

You! Everyone taking this book in their hands is special and deserves to be acknowledged.

Table of Contents

Introduction 1

PART I: Circumstances of Life 4

Chapter One: From Trials to Blessings.....................7

Chapter Two: My Faith at Work............................11

PART II: As it is Spoken, so My Life is........................... 15

Chapter Three: The Powerful Tongue 17

Chapter Four: Shaped 21

Chapter Five: The Power of Prayer 24

Chapter Six: The Book of James 30

Chapter Seven: The Valley Experience vs The Mountain Top..37

Epilogue/Conclusion... 41

Acknowledgments... 44

About the Author 46

v

Introduction

Congratulations! You have made a step into your walk with Jesus Christ. This book is centered on the Epistle of James in the Holy Bible. Reading, meditating, praying and letting the Holy Spirit speak to us freely. As humans, it can be hard to find direction or to remain in the right direction with all the trials of life. This book is a companion to you!

This book will be a reading companion for the book of James, with this book, you will read the entire Book of James chapter by chapter. Through these readings, we will pray the word of God together. You will find several prayer points that will lead you into deep moments of prayer that will lead to inevitable encounters, revelations, deliverance and more…and all that for the Glory of God.

This is not a how-to manual. It is not a quick fix but it is a companion. Why a companion, the word of God states, where two or three are gathered in my name, I am amongst them. There is no reference to distance or time, meaning that wherever you are and whatever the time. Together we will read, pray and conquer for the glory of God. It may be the first time you pick up one of my books, or the first time you and I will spend time in prayer together. I thank the Lord for His Grace over my life and the instruction to push out what He had put in me. Over the years, the decades, trials have come my way and taught me to cling on to the Lord and here we are today, MORE THAN A CONQUEROR.

Grab a physical bible, grab a pen and paper and let us merge into the word of God in the book of James. Whether you are alone or in a group, you are not just alone, the Holy Spirit is also there and ready to side by you.

It is by the word of their testimony that they overcame, I know that through these moments, you will encounter a lot of Blessings from the Lord, testify and share with every soul that is near and close to you.

PART I: Circumstances of Life

James 1 vs 2 to 8 - My brethren, count it all joy when you fall into various trials, knowing that the *testing of your faith produces patience.* But let patience have its perfect work, that you may be perfect and complete, lacking nothing. If any of you lacks wisdom, let him ask of God, who gives to all liberally and without reproach, and it will be given to him. But let him ask in faith, with no doubting, for he who doubts is like a wave of the sea driven and tossed by the wind. For let not that man suppose that he will receive anything from the Lord; *he is a double-minded man, unstable in all his ways.*

James 1 vs 12, 13 and 18 – *Blessed* is the man who *endures temptation*; for when he has been approved, he will receive the *crown of life which the Lord has promised to those who love Him. _God cannot be tempted by evil, nor does He Himself tempt anyone. _ Every good gift and every perfect gift is from above, and comes down from the Father of lights, with whom there is no variation or shadow of turning.*

James 1 vs 19, 22, 25 and 27 - ...*be swift to hear, slow to speak, slow to wrath;_ But be doers of the word, and not hearers only, deceiving yourselves. _ But he who looks into the perfect law of liberty and continues in it, and is not a forgetful hearer but a does of the work, this one will be blessed in what he does. Pure and undefiled religion before God and the Father is this: to visit orphans and widows in their trouble, and to keep oneself unspotted from the world.*

Change Your Life – Living the Wisdom of The Word

Chapter One: From Trials to Blessings

The Chapter begins with what most of us do not expect in life. "Count it all joy when you fall into various trials!" In the midst of a trial, we are directed to take it with joy. Not just a specific, but various trials, all sort of trials, whether be health, finance, marital, educational and the list goes on.

Your trials will not discourage you from following Jesus Christ. Your trials will not trigger sorrow but will engage you into long-lasting joy, In the name of Jesus. Your trials, will generate a pathway for you to celebrate the Joy of being with Jesus.

Take this moment, to declare upon your life.

In the name of Jesus, my trials will not obscure me but raise me in Joy because I know it is my faith in works.

My faith may be small as a mustard seed but in the name of Jesus, my FAITH produces patience. No trial on earth will push me around, I receive divine patience from my FAITH in the name of Jesus.

It is interesting how we are aware that Solomon after being sworn in King, does not waste his time asking for fame, power and victories but he asks for wisdom and here again, the apostle reminds us of the importance of asking. It is okay to lack, in the sense that we come with imperfections and lacks of various nature, however, it is not okay not to ask. You are set, created and in a position where you should lack nothing! You are complete in the name of Jesus.

Oh Lord, I am lacking wisdom, give me wisdom that I may walk in wisdom that may share wisdom, for your glory.

In the name of Jesus, away from me any doubt, any uncertainties.

In the name of Jesus, I am grounded in God, I will not be moved like waves of the sea.

In the name of Jesus, the winds of life will not toss me around. I am stable in all my ways.

I am Blessed in the name of Jesus. In the name of Jesus I receive my gifts from my father above.

Oh Lord, craft my character, craft me to be swift to hear.

Oh Lord, craft my character, craft me to be slow to speak.

Oh Lord, craft my character, craft me to be slow to wrath.

Oh Lord, give me the qualities needed in trials.

In the name of Jesus, I am a doer of the word of God, the word that will never pass.

Oh Lord my God, bless me father, bless me Oh Lord.

In the name of Jesus, we have prayed. In the name of Jesus, through this prayer, we receive a divine visitation and revelation that will propel us and establish us.

Chapter Two: My Faith at Work

BELIEVE! Yes, you NEED to believe, you MUST believe! In James 2 vs 23 and 25 the scriptures reads – And the Scripture was fulfilled which says, "Abraham believed God, and it was accounted to him for righteousness." And he was called the friend of God. _ Likewise, was not Rahab the harlot also justified by works when she received the messengers and sent them out another way?

And if we take a step back in verse 24 the word reads – You see then that a man is justified by works, and not by faith only.

It is important to note that Abraham was presented with situations that no one had experienced in the past. He is first instructed by God to leave his entire family and go. He is then told that he will be the father of many nations, yet he is childless! When this happens there is no Ishmael and no Isaac in the picture, and he is not thinking about it due to his age and the one of Sarah his wife.

To believe can be challenging, but a lot you went to high school, college and university. When you enrolled you firmly believed that you'd graduate and earn your diploma, degree, and certificate. What made you believe?

In this digital world, you log online and see your bank accounts with the funds in it. You go to merchants and confidently swipe for the amount you can afford because you believe that the funds are there and the transaction will go through.

What makes you believe?

The same way the word says faith without works is dead, if you did not get an admission into the educational institution, if you did not get a deposit into your bank account; you would have said I am not sure I can do it.

Likewise, put your faith at work, Hebrews Chapter 11 explains and breaks down faith in the best most perfect way. Not just verse 1 to 3 but the entire Chapter. Faith is the substance, it is the element, and it is the main thing of things hoped for, the evidence of things not seen…By faith, we understand how the world was created, by faith Abel offered…, by faith Enoch was taken…, by faith Noah, being divinely warned…, by faith Abraham obeyed…, by faith Sarah herself also received strength…, by faith Abraham, when he was tested…, by faith Isaac blessed Jacob…, by faith Moses…by faith David…by faith You will…By faith you are…

In the name of Jesus, my faith is put to work.

In the name of Jesus, my faith is not dormant, my faith is active and at work.

In the name of Jesus, as Abraham believed, I believe in God.

In the name of Jesus, as it was accounted for Abraham, it is accounted to me by God.

In the name of Jesus, my faith will not be plundered nor die.

In the name of Jesus my faith is perfecting itself.

My faith generates works in the name of Jesus.

In the name of Jesus, by faith I will offer good sacrifices to the Lord.

In the name of Jesus, I diligently seek God continuously, not just for a season.

In the name of Jesus, by faith I will receive divine warning of things not yet seen in my family and my generation.

In the name of Jesus, by faith I will respond to the call of the Lord when He calls me.

In the name of Jesus, by faith I pass through every trial and uncomfortable situation.

Change Your Life – Living the Wisdom of The Word

PART II: As it is Spoken, so My Life is

Change Your Life – Living the Wisdom of The Word

Chapter Three: The Powerful Tongue

In the beginning, God created the Heaven and the Earth. Then God said…Meaning God spoke words, and these words created things during 7 days as each day is detailed to us in the book of Genesis.

Death and life are in the power of the tongue, And those who love it will eat its fruit (Proverbs 18:21).

James 3 vs 9 and 11 _ With it we bless our God and Father, and with it we curse men, who have been made in the similitude of God. Out of the same mouth proceed blessing and cursing. _ Does a spring send forth fresh water and bitter from the same opening?

Indeed, these words can seem simple but yet if taken into consideration, which you ought to do, we see that our character will be one of first class. By continuously speaking life with our tongue, we who have been created according to God's image will be speaking constant life, deliverance, blessing into lives. Let us take for example a married couple, they love each other, speak encouragement, compliment to each other and then the same two, because of misunderstanding, begin to curse and insult, diminish, discourage with the same tongue. Hence James 3 vs 12 asks us a very good question _ Can a fig tree, my brethren bear olives, or a grapevine bear figs?

Let us strive to continuously speak life and bless all who we encounter.

In the name of Jesus, my tongue is restored. In the name of Jesus, I will not speak death, I will not curse but I shall speak love and life.

In the name of Jesus, I will speak peace always. I declare the character of peace to flourish out of me.

In the name of Jesus, I will speak righteousness, I declare the character of righteousness to flourish out of me.

In the name of Jesus, any residue of bitterness settled in me, be purged out of my character, out of me.

In the name of Jesus, any residue of envy settled in me, be purged out of my character, my life! Out of me in the name of Jesus.

In the name of Jesus, any demonic activity at work in my character be gone!

In the name of Jesus, any demonic activity pushing me to be at comfort with lying, boasting, be gone!

In the name of Jesus, any demonic activity pushing me into hypocrisy, be gone!

In the name of Jesus, the fruit of righteousness is at work in my life, in my destiny. Oh Lord, my God, let the good fruits of righteousness flourish in me.

In the name of Jesus, my tongue will build up all those it meets.

In the name of Jesus, my tongue will not destroy but create.

In the name of Jesus, my tongue is an empowering tool.

In the name of Jesus, my tongue is an instrument of Blessing, Praise and Worship.

In the name of Jesus, my tongue will comfort.

Chapter Four: Shaped

James 4 is centered on the behavior of one. SHAPED for a better lifestyle. Shaped to walk in truth and integrity. How can you not ask exactly for what you need? If we saw earlier that God says_ Ask for Wisdom, it will be given to the one who asks. Yet again, we ask amiss that we may spend it on pleasures. (Vs 3). As a child, you do not need to ask for car, for a house, for shiny precious metals!

Ask on target, ask for the wisdom that will enable you to manage your finances the right way, which in return will put you in a position where you can purchase a house, the fancy car, and the precious metals. We tend to forget that the world was created by the intelligence and wisdom of God. As a father, He is willing to pass it on to us, there is no need to wonder if such is possible because it is.

King Solomon asked and he received it. Daniel received so much wisdom that he was such an important and major influence. Coming back to our example in Chapter 1. We say I will graduate, I will buy, and I will take that vacation! Oh, let us be shaped and aligned with the word of God. Let us shift our lifestyle into a godly and anointed lifestyle. If the Lord wills, we shall live and graduate from college, from university.

Oh Lord my God, destroy any mountain of pride in me.

In the name of Jesus, any evil spirit that has made of my life its habitation, be GONE!

In the name of Jesus, I submit to God. My character submits to God, My life submits to God. My soul submits to God.

Oh Lord my God, empower me to resist the devil in every circumstance.

In the name of Jesus, Lord I need you with me always.

Oh Lord my God, touch me.

Oh Lord my God, hold me near and in you always.

Oh Lord my God, shape me to reflect your wisdom.

Change Your Life – Living the Wisdom of The Word

Chapter Five: The Power of Prayer

James 5 vs 13 to 15 – Is anyone among you suffering? Let him pray. Is anyone cheerful? Let him sing psalms. Is anyone among you sick? Let him call for the elders of the church, and let them pray over him, anointing him with oil in the name of the Lord. And the prayer of faith will save the sick, and the Lord will raise him up. And if he has committed sins, he will be forgiven.

In this chapter, we see the Power of Prayer, the Patience in Trials, The Perils of Wealth and Power, the Care for the Vulnerable, the Integrity in Speech and Actions, Restoring the Wander, Living out of Faith.

However, today we are diving in The Power of Prayer. We see the different types prayers: Prayers in Suffering, prayers in Joy and Prayers for Healing. You need to position yourself and understand that Prayer is Power, hence, you need to cultivate a consistent prayer life!

Communicate, talk with God, with the Holy Spirit. This is done through what is called prayer. In prayer, you pour out your heart to God Almighty. We see the Power of Prayer because it exposes the situation and gives the solution – PRAY.

PRAY, PRAy, PRay, Pray, pray, praY, prAY, pRAY, PRAY!

If you have a trial, a situation, a challenge through which you are going through today, you are at loss of words, you are seeking answers, seeking a solution. The solution comes by prayer, the power that prayer carries will generate a pressure that unclogs what is not flowing in your life. I speak to you out of personal experience. This is not a generic text but a practical word to you. My life has been transformed, my character has been transformed. With prayer, I have experienced healing, not only physical but emotional healing too. Through prayer, I have received direction, through prayer, I have received comfort.

Does prayer really have power? Is prayer something real or is it a myth that people use to seem important or something? I was there too, asking myself the same questions, asking why are people so hooked to prayer. My curiosity arose when I realized that the disciples did not ask Jesus, How do you make miracles happen? They asked Him: Lord, teach us to pray, as John also taught his disciples (Luke 11: 1 – 4). From there another question arose, another because I knew that I was unworthy. According to my judgment. How could I even try and pray. A life with every imperfection one could think of, yet the eagerness to pray kept knocking at the door of my heart. This is when I understood that Prayer is more than the word PRAYER. I understood that there is Power in Prayer, that there is an incredible deep, profound mystery in prayer.

In Prayer and with faith, we call things to existence, we cancel things that should not be. God created the

Heavens and Earth through speech. By speaking. God also created the human spices the same way and blessed the human and declared that we will be like His image. The Lord has given you the authority over the enemy (Satan). The key to access into the spiritual realm and alter things back to the way they ought to be as we read earlier is to Pray. Your prayers will heal, deliver, restore and establish.

The lack and negligence of prayer can derail and destroy an entire destiny. What is a destiny? It is the events that will necessarily happen to a particular person. It is the hidden power believed to control what will happen in the future. (This definition is from the dictionary, look it up, google it and see.) Now, necessarily means inevitably which means unavoidable. You cannot avoid going into your destiny whether it is corrupted, damaged, altered or in its original state. Can you preserve your God established destiny? By yourself, you can never succeed, however with prayer you can.

Can your God given destiny be corrupted, altered, attacked, and damaged? Yes, if you do not care for it. The enemy makes it a playground. You see the spiritual realm is very interesting, and the only way to access it, for us children of God is via prayer. Your body cannot enter that dimension, however, your soul, your spirt can go and seat at the table, can go on the battle ground. As you are here on earth, your prayer life is the asset, the weapon that you use. No one can take prayer away from you except you! You do not want to pray, it's on you. You want to leave a life of defeat? It is easy, seat back and relax and keep prayer out of your life. Don't take having a nice fancy car, a mansion, designer clothes, accessories and the lavish lifestyle, the degrees as the success of life, as the happiness of life.

Today, you will see that atheist, Satanists and all other beliefs here on hearth have a form of way to access the spiritual realm, it is either by the means of meditation, yoga, rituals etc… it is to show you that their spirit needs to be one attended to and that they understood that things are done in the spirit realm.

Now, as a Christian, we know that we are in the army of the Lord. Our Lord Jesus Christ conquered the grave, Satan was defeated and has never and will never win a battle against the army of the Lord. We also know that the kingdom of Heaven is attacked on a daily basis by our common enemy Satan and his troops (principalities and demons).

The Power of Prayer is your arsenal.

In the name of Jesus, I arise in prayer.

In the name of Jesus, the Lord is my guardian, the guardian of my destiny.

In the name of Jesus, I am saved from all sickness.

Oh Lord my God, raise me up for your glory.

Oh Lord my God, forgive me of my sins.

My father, in the name above every name, restore my destiny.

Oh speak to me Lord, reveal your will oh Lord God.

Oh Lord, my life is calling you for a divine visitation and intervention.

In the name of Jesus, I speak to any altar erected to destroy me, and I call onto the Lord of Abraham, Isaac and Jacob, The God whom answers by fire to answer as he did on Mount Zerubbabel. Evil altars battling my life and destiny, BE SILENCED.

In the name of Jesus, evil patterns established in my destiny; break, terminate.

In the name of Jesus, my destiny is restored.

Change Your Life – Living the Wisdom of The Word

Chapter Six: The Book of James

Genuine faith endures trials. These come but you have to be strong. With a strong faith you will face the trials head-on, and build up lasting endurance in the process.

Genuine faith comprehends temptations. Lust will not find its way in and hence not permitting you to slide into sin. The power of sin was broken by Christ through His death and resurrection.

Genuine faith ports no prejudice. Faith and favoritism cannot coexist. Hatred and bitterness against another have no place in the kingdom of God.

Genuine faith has the power to control the tongue. Words are extremely powerful; this is also a reminder that words of Grace bring life and encouragement.

Genuine faith acts wisely. It empowers you to choose heavenly wisdom that brings life. Reject earthly wisdom that brings death.

Genuine faith produces separation from the world and submission to God. Resist the devil and humbly draw closer to god.

Genuine faith waits patiently for the coming of the Lord. Trials and troubles do not discourage us.

A key element to take from James, is that even when you feel the most comfortable with the Lord – even when you believe you have Him figured out – The Lord can still surprise you and change your world.

After reading the book of James, one must strive to become A Changed person. When we take a deeper approach into every chapter and verse we see unconditional and life changing lessons. Do not put your bible down just yet, take it with a highlighter and a note pad to take down notes. In the first chapter, we receive instructions in regards to trials:

Verse 2 – There is nothing joyful about trials. The key to finding joy in adversity is where we place focus. However, when you fix your eyes on Jesus, you will learn to rejoice in your difficulty because God has promised to work through them to strengthen your Faith, and brings you into a closer fellowship with Him and teaches you endurance.

Verse 3 – When you face trials, there is one thing you need not to doubt, and that is GOD IS PRODUCING SOMETHING EXCELLENT in YOU. Take time to turn completely to the Lord and experience Joy, Comfort, Power and Assurance. You need not to react to trials with emotions but respond with faith in the Lords perfect provision.

Verse 5 – We all need to ask God for Wisdom. With wisdom, you will have the ability to see life from God's point of view. God will never deny giving you wisdom. Do not shy out and not ask for it.

Verse 13 – There is a thing about humans, a big misinterpretation of facts. It is critical to know that God is Holy and would never tempt anyone to do evil because that is not His character. Do not blame or let anyone lead you in the direction of blaming God for bad behavior or lust.

Verse 14 and 15 – The enemy is wicked and crooked. This is why he will tempt you to sin. That is to prevent you from obeying God and experience the best of God. The devil has an agenda to do anything he can to enslave you to do things that will wreck and destroy your effectiveness for the kingdom of God. Do not be discouraged, however, because you have the power through Jesus Christ to say no to his wicked schemes.

Verse 17 – Everything has a source. God is the source of every good thing we have. Look at everything you already have; he was faithful to provide it. No need to worry about the future. He will not change.

Verse 22 – Obedience is not easy. Obey, obey and obeying is not easy. Obeying the word of God is not always an easy task. Be reassured that the Lord understands the difficulty and challenge of it. Our task is to obey God and allow Him to handle the rest. Apply the principles of God to your life and you find victory over sin and death.

Verse 27 – Allow God to transform you into His image so you may increasingly reflect His love and compassionate character upon you. Do not neglect your relationship with God, do not disobey His commands.

In the second chapter, we receive a deeper edification on the nature of true faith:

Verse 1 – Every human walking on this earth is loved by God. Jesus Christ sacrificed Himself on the cross to save everyone. Your neighbors, the people you meet on the bus, the people you see at the market, on the road, in other countries…everyone

Verse 5 – Being rich or wealthy here on earth does not and will never equal spiritual wealth.

Verse 10 – Good enough! There is only one way to be good enough, and that is to earn salvation or the grace of God. You must fully and completely be obedient to God by accepting Christ.

Verse 15 to 16 – Love, the Love of God is deeper than any love man can try and explain or give out. The good thing, faith in God will transform a person's character and behavior and push that person to love unconditionally. Obeying God and serving others as per the will of God.

Verse 18 – Seeking Jesus, knowing Jesus is something all must strive for. When you begin to identify as one who knows Jesus, there must also be a confirmation in your life that the Holy Spirit is crafting you into likeness of Christ. A legitimate and positive change.

In the third chapter, we are enlightened on the tongue and heavenly wisdom:

Verse 5 – The powerful tongue we all have. The spoken words, the tongue has power that can set the course of your own life and those around you. You cannot hide, your sinful ways will be revealed by what you say. I urge again, pray that Jesus may sanctify and transform you from the inside out.

Verse 16 – Do not envy others. When you begin to go down that route, know that the enemy was successful on taking your focus away from God. Once you become distracted, covetous and prideful, the enemy is rejoicing because he knows it will prevent you to enjoy the Blessings of God.

Verse 17 – The wisdom acquired from God leads to harmony and peace. Yet, the wisdom of humans leads to arrogance and disagreement.

In the fourth chapter, a teaching on pride versus humility:

Verse 4 – Live for the Lord. Yes, My Life for Jesus. When you do so, light shines over you and it convicts those who do not.

Verse 7 – Temptation by the enemy is a daily routine. The enemy can use the prideful route. Making you seek for your own success rather than God. There is a way to resist at it and that is by submitting ourselves to Christ. Accept the wisdom and will of God. Trust His power and love as you obey His command.

Verse 10 – The formula is Submit yourself fully to the Lord and let Him work through you to achieve His will.

Verse 17 – You do not do the will of God, You sin against God. Obey the Lord and be reassured and know that you are blessed for your obedience.

In the fifth chapter, it is filled with equipment to live. Warning to the Rich, persevering patience and much more:

Verse 7 – Stay the course and endure it. Be patient! Stay away from rage no matter what the circumstance is. Trust God always.

Verse 10 – Adversity is an opportunity for you to see the Power of God and all is Love. It will release you from bondages you may not be aware of.

Verse 17 – Fervent prayer pf a righteous man avails much. Trust God like Prophet Elijah, prompt answers to his requests.

Change Your Life – Living the Wisdom of The Word

Chapter Seven: The Valley Experience vs The Mountain Top

My brethren, take the prophets, who spoke in the name of the Lord, as an example of suffering and patience. (James 5 vs 10).

There are a few questions we will address, some of these questions came up during bible studies and during fellowship.

A lot of people say adversity reveals our level of Faith, is it really written in the bible? *Yes, it is written in the bible in the book of Mark 4: 35 – 41.* Faith says that God is in control. Looking at 3 statements from these scriptures:

- Let us cross over to the other side (vs. 35)

- Teacher, do You not care that we are perishing? (vs. 38)

- Why are you fearful? How is it that you have no faith? (vs. 40)

God has given you the ability to trust Him. With the trust, you are set to overcome fear, anxiety and doubt. Adversity should be a mechanism to shoot your faith into Action and not into questioning or doubt. It will prompt you to act with confidence and generate a faith growth in you.

Can adversity really reveal our strengths and weaknesses? *Yes and the confirmation to that is in the book of Judges 6: 11 – 24.* You are strong! You are righteous! You are forgiven! Your strength resides in the Lord and not in you or any other source. As His children, we are granted access and privileged to tap into His power.

- The Lord is with you, you mighty man of valor (vs. 12)

- my lord, if the Lord is with us, why then has all this happened to us (vs. 13)

- But now the Lord has forsaken us (vs. 13)

- Go in this might of yours, and you shall save Israel from the hand of the Midianites. Have I not sent you? (vs. 14)

- Indeed my clan is the weakest in Manasseh, and I am the least in my father's house. (vs. 15)

- Surely I will be with you, and you shall defeat the Midianites as one man. (vs. 16)

As we journey through life, we find ourselves in various situation, some favorable and some not. Life questions you and you question life as well as to why me? Why this? Why that?

Why do I have to face constant criticism, and it seems to increase when I am in the so-called valley going through challenges?

"But he said to her, "You speak as one of the foolish women speaks. Shall we indeed accept good from God, and shall we not accept adversity?" Job 2 vs. 10.

Like Job, we are to stand firm in our faith. The Lord Jesus Christ won the battle of battles. That is on the Cross. That victory is within you today. Pray unto the Lord, and ask for faith and hope.

In all and all, we all want a successful outcome. Now is there a roadmap, is there a formula? A key pattern to observe is the one of Moses in the book of Exodus 3: 1 – 4: Unlike what we all assume, that there is a formula to success, do this and that and you will see. Humans are used to single one formula to make it happen. However, as a child of God, know that the Lord is beyond innovative.

Change Your Life – Living the Wisdom of The Word

Epilogue/Conclusion

God is good all the time and all the time God is good. I pray that you continue to pray and not take your prayer life casually. Read the word of God and pray the word of God.

The enemy cannot and will not dominate you. Our father, has established you on earth to be His ambassador and will not forsake you. The mandate you have been given, the purpose for which you are here on earth, in your family, in your household can only be maintained with a dedicated prayer life.

1. Draw near to God and He will draw near to you (James 4 vs 8).

2. And the Prayer of faith will save the sick, and the Lord will raise him up. And if he has committed sins, he will be forgiven. (James 5 vs 15).

3. You also be patient. Establish your hearts, for the coming of the Lord is at hand. (James 5 vs 8).

4. If any of you lacks wisdom, let him ask God, who gives to all liberally and without reproach, and it will be given to him. (James 1 vs 5).

5. Blessed is the man who endures temptation; for when he has been approved, he will receive the crown of life which the Lord has promised to those who love Him. (James 1 vs 12).

6. Therefore submit to God. Resist the devil and he will flee from you. (James 4 vs 7).

If God is never too busy for you? How can you be too busy to pursue your earthly dreams when the breath of life that you have is not even under your control!

May God Bless you.

Change Your Life – Living the Wisdom of The Word

Acknowledgments

Thank you, Lord Jesus, for thy presence.

Thank you to you, as you seek the Lord and share the gospel with every soul you meet. Thank you for sharing this booklet with those you know and those you do not know.

Thank you to you Joelle, through the ups and downs. In prayer always we remain. The battles are real and the victory is more real.

Thank you to my three princesses- Eliana, Emilia and Eva, every day as I see you guys, I testify that God is faithful. Daddy loves you guys.

Thank you Pastor Paul Militsala, may the Lord continue to anoint you, thank you for all the teachings that you have poured into me and many others.

Thank you Rev. Joseph Aryeequaye, the prayer watch sessions have built and deepened my thirst for the prayer and studying the word of God.

Thank you Apostle Debbie Banda-Viggs, the mentorship, the friendship, forever grateful I will be.

Papa Eli and Maman Rosalie Tshibwabwa (My beloved Parents) thank you for taking the time to teach me how to read and write. May God Bless you more and always.

Thank you, Lord, for the prayer mantle that you have clothed me with.

Shalom.

About the Author

Blaise Tshibwabwa, a respected author, motivational speaker, and minister, leverages his extensive ministry experience to create impactful contributions that inspire and uplift individuals seeking guidance and spiritual enlightenment.

Renowned for his profound books like "The Power of Union" and "Plan 2 B U," Blaise's writings are deeply rooted in biblical teachings, offering practical guidance for navigating life's challenges and embracing a purpose-driven existence.

Beyond writing, Blaise's philanthropic efforts in charitable endeavors, particularly with orphanages, showcase his commitment to positively impacting the lives of those in need, resonating with individuals and communities striving to create a better world for all.

Blaise's talent as a public speaker further amplifies his ability to inspire audiences of all ages and backgrounds, motivating them to embrace their potential, pursue their dreams, and overcome obstacles with unwavering resilience. His speeches catalyze personal and spiritual growth, empowering listeners to lead fulfilling lives.

Blaise Tshibwabwa's impactful words can ignite personal and spiritual growth. Through his ministry, writing, and speaking, he empowers listeners to bring positive change to their lives and communities. His profound contributions are evident in his unwavering commitment to spreading hope, positivity, and biblical truths.

Blaise's enduring legacy inspires and motivates generations, leaving a lasting impression on all who engage with his work.

www.ingramcontent.com/pod-product-compliance
Lightning Source LLC
Chambersburg PA
CBHW070802050426
42452CB00012B/2455